LIBRARY TRAINING GUIDES

Series Editor: David Baker
Editorial Assistant: Joan Welsby

Introduction by the Series Editor

This new series of Library Training Guides (LTGs for short) aims to fill the gap left by the demise of the old Training Guidelines published in the 1980s in the wake of the Library Association's work on staff training. The new LTGs develop the original concept of concisely written summaries of the best principles and practice in specific areas of training by experts in the field which give library and information workers a good-quality guide to best practice. Like the original guidelines, the LTGs also include appropriate examples from a variety of library systems as well as further reading and useful contacts.

Though each guide stands in its own right, LTGs form a coherent whole. Acquisition of all LTGs as they are published will result in a comprehensive manual of training and staff development in library and information work.

The guides are aimed at practising librarians and library training officers. They are intended to be comprehensive without being over-detailed; they should give both the novice and the experienced librarian/training officer an overview of what should/could be done in a given situation and in relation to a particular skill/group of library staff/type of library.

David Baker

LIBRARY TRAINING GUIDES

Evaluation

Steven Phillips

Library Association Publishing

© Library Association Publishing Ltd 1993

Published by
Library Association Publishing Ltd
7 Ridgmount Street
London WC1E 7AE

First published 1993
Reprinted 1995

British Library Cataloguing in Publication Data. A catalogue record for this book is available from the British Library.

ISBN 1-85604-079-8

Typeset in 11/12pt Palermo from author's disk by Library Association Publishing Ltd
Printed and made in Great Britain by The Looseleaf Company, Melksham, Wiltshire.

Contents

Summary

This guide looks at the evaluation of training. It examines how librarians can manage the process of training to be clear about what is intended as an objective. It also looks at how to assess the training both to ensure its quality and appropriateness and to evaluate the actual outcome. This can then be compared to the intention, and either the training or the original objective can be amended in the light of the results.

Evaluation is part of the training cycle and should be a continuing process which informs all parts of the cycle. It therefore needs to be considered in the planning of training, and not just added as an afterthought.

Different levels of outcome result from staff participating in training. These range from changes in attitude and learning by the individuals taking part, through changes in individual behaviour, to changes in organizational behaviour. The various levels require different approaches in gathering information. Generally speaking, it is easiest to ascertain information about individual perceptions, more difficult to identify learning and changes in individual behaviour, and most difficult to link changes in the performance of an organization to a programme of training. In addition it is generally easier to obtain quantitative information about activities than it is to measure qualitative changes.

Managers of libraries, and indeed of many other types of organization, generally have not made great use of the evaluation of training. This is both because, as indicated above, the more useful information is hard to obtain, and because in an environment of tight budgets evaluation is in itself a resource-consuming process.

This guide recognizes the difficulties and tries to identify both when it is appropriate to evaluate training, and also practical methods with which evaluation can be undertaken. It is not a complete exposition of all the ways in which training can be evaluated, but gives an indication of the approaches which might work in various circumstances.

Acknowledgements

Thanks are due to the many people who gave their time in explaining the approach of their particular organization to the evaluation of training, and who passed on examples of documents. In particular Sarah Hassan and Trevor Wadlow of Norfolk County Council, Rebecca Goldsmith of Cambridgeshire Library & Information Service, and David Evans of City College, Norwich should be thanked.

Thanks are also due to the following organizations for giving permission to reproduce the forms in the appendix. Norfolk County Council (examples 1, 3, 7); Suffolk County Council Arts & Libraries Department (example 2); City College, Norwich (examples 4, 10); National Training Index (examples 5, 6, 8); West Suffolk College (example 9); Anglia Polytechnic University (examples 11, 12). Forms 2, 11 and 12 are in the process of revision.

1 Introduction

1.1 This guide will examine the evaluation of training. Evaluation is a process which can and should be applied to every area of library management to ensure that activities and outcomes are both appropriate and as intended. The principles are equally applicable to the development and delivery of training as they are to any other process. Indeed, training is a resource-intensive activity and as such is particularly deserving of attention to ensure that expenditure has been worthwhile.

1.2 Despite much theoretical writing about the evaluation of training the practice in libraries is often rudimentary or even non-existent. This is, to a large extent, because it is difficult to determine the causal links between training activity and subsequent organizational or individual behaviour. Undertaking the sophisticated data collection and analysis which can illuminate the real consequences of training programmes will often require a high level of resources in itself. Evaluation of training can therefore be both complicated and costly.

1.3 The literature relating to the management and delivery of training in general gives many examples of evaluation. Some of these techniques are applicable in libraries. Others rely on the organization involved having specific financial targets against which the effects of training can be measured; sales targets for example. These are often not so useful as indicators in library settings, though ascribing financial values to given outcomes of library service is one approach to the measurement of activity. Information services which exist in a commercial environment may well find them more useful.

1.4 The hesitancy of library managers to evaluate training is therefore understandable. It is often difficult to undertake, may involve a large commitment of resources, and techniques used in other settings appear to be inappropriate. Nevertheless, there are measures for deciding what can usefully be evaluated, and methods for doing it which do not require a disproportionate input of resources. This guide should be of use in describing what those measures and methods are.

Evaluation: what it is and why do it

2.1 The general purpose of evaluation is:

- to understand what is happening within an organization
- to assess the extent to which this matches what was intended to happen
- to indicate what decisions or actions need to be taken if there is a mismatch between the intention and the reality.

It is therefore part of a continuing wider management process of agreeing policies, formulating strategies to put these into practice, managing activities and assessing the effects of these activities.

2.2 As part of the cycle an organization needs to have a clear mission statement which includes strategic aims and objectives. This is an essential prerequisite of evaluation. There is no point in evaluating an activity unless there is agreement on its purpose. To be of practical use organizational objectives should include identifiable and measurable outcomes. A library mission statement which does not go beyond idealistic wishes to enrich the lives of its users is of no practical use either in determining management policy, or for providing benchmarks against which outcomes can be evaluated. For example, an objective might be the provision of an effective inter-library loan service. Within the resources available it may be decided that a target will be set such as: '90% of requests will be satisfied within ten working days'. This provides a benchmark against which standards of service can be measured.

2.3 Evaluation is undertaken for one, or more, of a number of reasons depending upon the particular need at the time, and the process or decision which is being considered. It can be a tool for understanding what is happening within an organization, and what is not. It can indicate changes which need to be made to enable objectives to be fulfilled. It may also contribute to a reconsideration of the original objectives if they appear to have been inappropriate or unattainable.

2.4 Accountability to a wider organization, or even an external agency, is a further purpose of evaluation. There may be a need for a manager to provide evidence of activity, particularly where funding has been made available for specific purposes. Performance indicators are increasingly being applied to provide 'snapshot' pictures of organizational performance, often introduced at the prompting of management consultants or auditors.

2.5 Evaluation can also be a means for enabling clients, sponsors and staff at all levels to participate in the management process. Various techniques can be used which allow all of these 'stakeholders', as they are sometimes called, to express opinions on both activities and their outcomes.

2.6 The term 'evaluation' carries an implication that an assessment of quality or value is being made. This is a key point. A distinction can be made between the measurement of quality and that of quantity. The two may well coincide, but it should not be assumed that this is the case. For example, the quantitative measure of the speed of delivery of interlibrary loans will usually also be qualitative, as a value can be put on the provision of such a service. In comparison, a single measurement of books loaned daily is unlikely to be qualitative because the reasons for providing such a service are much more diverse and often contradictory. The externally set performance indicators increasingly encountered are usually quantitative, often being measures of cost per unit of output or activity.

2.7 Quality is not measured on an absolute scale. It is a measure which takes into account the appropriateness of what is being examined. An activity which is ideal in one situation may be inappropriate in another. This must be considered when undertaking evaluation.

2.8 When assessing activities quality is also relative to the amount of resources which are available as an input. Libraries are never in a position of having unlimited funding, and activities have to optimize the services within the constraints of these resources. One general approach to the evaluation of training has been to apply the concepts of cost-effectiveness where the outcome of an activity is measured in terms of the input of resources. This will be considered in Chapter 7.

2.9 It is nearly always the case that evaluative assessments, to be meaningful, need to be relative measurements. That is, they should be expressed as one measurement in terms of another. Thus the registered number of users of a service is put into context when compared to the potential number. Measurement may also be relative over time, such as changes in levels of satisfaction.

3 The training cycle

3.1 Evaluation should be one part in a continuing process of formulation, delivery and review of training. The whole process is sometimes characterized as a recurring cycle of events described as the *cycle of training*. This will be referred to in other Training Guides in this series.

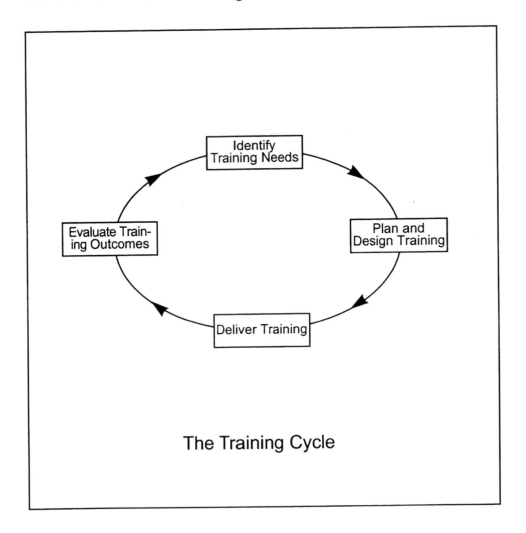

The Training Cycle

3.2 This diagram represents a generally accepted conceptual model of the training cycle, showing the context for evaluation. There are many other similar examples in the literature. It is worth discussing this model in some detail to put the different approaches and activities of evaluation into context.

3.3 The cycle begins with the identification of training needs. The strategic aims and the specific objectives of the organization should then be considered in detail. From these, the ways in which training and development can contribute to effective implementation of the objectives should be considered. This should be done with reference to both the intended development of the organization, and the abilities, skills and attitudes of the staff in post, as well as those likely to be recruited. There is a variety of techniques available to assess staff development needs, and some, such as staff development interviews, are themselves part of the evaluation process. The training needs within an organization are therefore a combination of both an agreed strategic development plan, and the aggregation of the specific needs of individuals and groups within the organization.

3.4 The identification of training needs is more than an exercise in listing all the areas where training would benefit an organization. In an environment where resources will always be limited it also involves a process of promoting a commitment to training amongst the managers, agreeing priorities, and obtaining the resources necessary to undertake training.

3.5 The next stage in the training cycle is the planning and design of training. This follows from the identification of training needs. At this stage a programme of training is drawn up, having identified specific intended outcomes, and what forms of training are most appropriate, both for the intended purpose and for the staff being trained. This will be done within the context of fixed resources, and will involve the development of an operational plan for delivering the training and development over a period of time. Again, this should be related both to the objectives of the organization and to the needs of the individuals. The planning and design stage includes the specification of learning programmes, materials and learner support; testing and adapting training programmes where these will be large-scale activities; and decisions on a variety of matters such as the suitability of particular qualifications or whether to use in-house facilities as opposed to external agencies to undertake the training.

3.6 The third stage in the cycle is the delivery of training. The delivery may be carried out directly by the organization or through outside agents, but in both cases the process needs to be managed to ensure effectiveness and quality. The activities in this stage include allocating and managing the resources obtained, preparation of learning materials, delivery of the training, and support for those who are taking part.

3.7 The last part of the cycle is the evaluation of the outcomes of the training undertaken. The results and effects are measured to assess what has actually happened within the organization. An assessment is also made of the perceptions by those involved of the content, structure and effectiveness of the activities. This information is compared to the objectives, both of the organization and of the stakeholders who have had an interest in the training activities. If the outcome matches the objective then the result is positive feedback. Discrepancy between intended outcomes and actual outcomes of the training, should lead to changes in the nature of the training activities, as they might have been inappropriate in themselves or ineffective for the staff involved. Alternatively there may be a reassessment of the original objectives. This then feeds back to the first identified part of the training cycle, and influences decisions about future training plans.

3.8 The common use of a circular model to illustrate how training should be conducted is deliberate. To function properly within an organization, training should be a continuing activity which responds to a changing environment and changing needs as well as to feedback about previous activity. Within this cycle the evaluation of training should also be a continuing process. Activities which are taking place throughout the year need to be monitored as they take place. Evaluation should also be taken into account as a part of all of the other stages in the training cycle. Whenever possible, activities should be formulated with evaluation of the outcome as one of the inputs to the design. Evaluation should take place during training as well as after so that if necessary the activity can be amended in the light of any feedback.

3.9 Organizations are increasingly adopting a cycle of interviewing and reporting on a regular basis, either as a means of informing and evaluating individual and organizational staff development programmes, or as part of a wider process of staff appraisal. The use of these helps to establish evaluation as a regular and continuing process which underlies all training activity.

Evaluation of training

4.1	The general issues of evaluation raised in Chapter 2 are all relevant to the evaluation of training. To put these into context:
4.1.1	Training should be designed to achieve organizational objectives, and these should be expressed in measurable outcomes where possible.
4.1.2	Evaluation of training should measure the outcomes of activity.
4.1.3	The outcomes should be compared to the original objectives.
4.1.4	If there is a disparity between objective and outcome there needs to be a re-examination of the style, quality or content of the training, the validity of the original objective, or the other factors affecting organizational performance in the work environment.
4.1.5	The quality of training is relative to the resources available for its provision, and evaluation should take account of this. Quality is also a measure of appropriateness and not an absolute. A training activity which is good in one situation may not work in another.
4.2	Before discussing the specific ways in which library training can be evaluated there are a number of points which need to be considered: putting the evaluation process into context, ensuring that the information obtained is relevant and useful, making effective use of the resources which will be needed to undertake the evaluation, and highlighting the particular difficulties which exist relating to development and training. It may seem negative to include a section on the problems involved, but a manager who will be using the techniques should be aware of the constraints. It was noted in Section 1.2 that, in practice, examples of evaluation are thin on the ground, and there are good reasons for this.
4.3	There are various different individuals and groups who have an interest in training, sometimes referred to as 'stakeholders'. These include the whole organization within which a library exists, the library itself, and its management. The senior staff of a library have an interest both as managers and as members of professional bodies. Others with an interest include the entire staff of the library, the deliverers of any training, professional organizations and the bodies which validate and award qualifications. The different interests and objectives of the stakeholders may not coincide, and may indeed conflict. Some examples should illustrate this.
4.4	A training plan may envisage a training activity – say The City & Guilds Certificate for Library Assistants – improving the performance of the staff who take part. The staff involved might see the activity as a way of

enhancing their prospects of promotion, or of obtaining a post in another organization. There will obviously be different expectations of outcomes. If the staff do obtain posts elsewhere, and the library has to recruit new untrained staff, the training activity will not have fulfilled its purpose for the organization.

4.5 The external agencies which are delivering training, whether they are colleges or consultants, will have their own objectives. These should include the delivery of quality, relevant training, but will undoubtedly also take in such matters as the immediate satisfaction of the participants with the training and the likelihood of further business being contracted with them. Again, there is the potential for a mismatch between the outcomes desired by the external agencies, and those of the library.

4.6 The problem in each of these cases is that the stakeholders should play an integral part in the evaluation process, but they may judge outcomes compared to their own objectives. Using the example from 4.4, staff who complete a course and then find that they do not achieve promotion may consider the training to have failed if that was their reason for taking part. At the same time the course may have resulted in improved job performance and thus have fulfilled the organizational objective. Similarly, evaluation results fed back from external agencies need to be treated with some scepticism.

4.7 The issue of a mismatch should not be a problem in that it is the needs of the organization which provide the stimulus, and in most cases the resources, for training. Although a training plan should take account of the views of other stakeholders, and may explicitly include consideration of individual or professional perspectives, the purpose of the training is to contribute to the achievement of agreed objectives, and evaluation should compare outcomes to those objectives. In the end the perceptions of stakeholders will be an invaluable part of the evaluation process, but managers need to be aware of the limitations of this source of feedback.

4.8 Another point which needs to be considered is the level at which activity is being evaluated. These can be grouped into the following broad areas:

- reactions and attitudes
- learning
- job behaviour
- organization and final outcome

4.9 Evaluation of reactions and attitudes assesses the perceptions of stakeholders to the training itself and is usually measured using questionnaires covering such matters as the content and delivery of the training. It is important because training is likely to be more effective if participants react positively to it, and participants will also be well placed to comment on its quality and suitability from their perspective.

4.10 The learning level refers to the effects on the individual of any particular training. This includes the knowledge which has been imparted, skills which have been developed, and attitudes which have been encouraged. Evaluation at this level is different from the measurement of reactions. Participants may feel positive about a training activity, for example because it took place in a comfortable environment or the trainer was interesting, but may even so have learned little. A variety of techniques to assess learning is available ranging from objective tests to attitude assessments. Learning is easier to measure if the objective is the transfer of a practical skill. Evaluation of learning is usually more involved than the evaluation of reactions and attitudes, and will thus require more sophisticated techniques and more resources. Evaluation of reactions to and the evaluation of learning arising from training, are important in assessing whether the content and form of the training are appropriate and effective.

4.11   The job behaviour level refers to the practical effect that training has had in the performance of tasks. Again, evaluation of job behaviour differs from that of the other levels. Even if a member of staff has demonstrably learned a particular skill, it does not follow that this skill will be put into practice. Outcomes of training in terms of individual behaviour need to be measured in the work environment, using techniques such as observation, and monitoring output.

4.12   The ultimate aim of the evaluation in the training cycle is to assess effects at the organizational level. It does not necessarily follow that a change in individual behaviour will result in the intended organizational outcome, and even when it appears to, it is particularly difficult to establish a causal link between such changes and any training which has taken place. Nevertheless, evaluation at this level is important for determining the outcome of training activity, for decisions on whether the objectives of the training have been fulfilled, and whether those objectives need to be revised in the light of outcomes. Assessment of this level of activity involves the application of measures which assess processes and outputs in terms of cost-benefit measures, performance indicators, or general evaluation of organizational performance.

4.13   The objectives for which activity is being undertaken should be expressed in terms of measurable outcomes. If organizational objectives are relatively intangible then it will be difficult to assess whether they have been achieved. However, even given a clear set of objectives and methods for determining organizational change, it is often extremely difficult to identify specific outcomes as the result of particular training activities. The human side of organizations is usually the most difficult to analyse, given the complicated and illogical behaviour sometimes exhibited by people.

4.14   Consider, for example, a library which institutes a programme of customer care training for the staff who have contact with users. User surveys might subsequently show improved perceptions of the friendliness and helpfulness of staff. Unfortunately, a number of alternative explanations might also be plausible for such an improvement. Personality clashes or personal problems of the staff involved might have been resolved; working conditions or rotas may have changed; supervisory staff may have been replaced. These or other reasons might equally well explain an improvement in staff effectiveness as perceived by users. The 'Hawthorne' effect is sometimes referred to where, following a study, the performance of employees was shown to improve when an interest was shown in their activities, even if no practical changes were made to their working arrangements.

4.15 It is more difficult to relate outcomes to the effects of general training. For example, some programmes have as their aim the raising of awareness of issues, such as race or gender at work. Except in cases where there has been obvious discrimination there will be little tangible evidence of behaviour over time which can be directly linked to training activities.

4.16 To be useful, evaluation of training can therefore be complex and time-consuming. It will be necessary to decide when it is appropriate to expend resources on this activity, and to what level evaluation should be carried. There are several factors to be considered in these decisions.

4.16.1 The value of the outcome to the organization is relevant. The more important the objective, the greater the need to evaluate and be clear whether it has been achieved.

4.16.2 It is also more important to evaluate activities which are going to be repeated than those which are one-off, though this does not imply that discrete activities should never be evaluated.

4.16.3 It is important to monitor any training undertaken by an external provider, as well as activities which are similar in nature to those likely to be undertaken in the future.

4.16.4 The cost of training is an important factor. There is a danger in underestimating costs, for example by not including the salaries of staff involved. Balanced against all of these is the cost of undertaking the evaluation.

Overall, the more important, expensive and frequently repeated the training activity, the greater the need to evaluate it.

5 Information for evaluation

5.1 The stages in the training cycle of identification of training needs, and the planning, design and delivery of training will be dealt with in other Training Guides in this series. Similarly, the formulation of mission statements including aims and objectives will be found covered in a number of general and library-specific management texts. However, mission statements may make only passing reference to training or staff development. The purpose of training is to assist in the achievement of the wider organizational objectives. To use the example of interlibrary loans from Section 2.2, if a target of satisfying requests within a time-scale is not being met, training might be identified as a potential solution. In this case the evaluation of the training activity will focus on whether it enabled the staff to fulfil the service target. This guide will assume that these points have been considered, and that training has been planned and delivered in the context of agreed measurable objectives. This and the following chapters will concentrate on the collection of information for the evaluation of training which can be compared to these objectives.

5.2 Two main decisions have to be made in the planning of evaluation. The first of these is which person or group should undertake the information-gathering, and the second is what information needs to be gathered.

5.3 The issue of who undertakes the process of evaluation and gathers the necessary information is important. There is a risk that responses to questions may vary depending on who is asking them. There are several reasons for this.

5.4 The person gathering the information is likely to be a stakeholder, and have some kind of interest in the outcome of the activity. It has already been indicated that individuals may have their own objectives in promoting, or taking part in, an activity, and these may not coincide with those of the organization. Examples of this are external organizations providing training which need to generate further business, and cases where individuals being trained would have liked a different outcome from that intended by the organization. The influences, however, may be more subtle than these. Activity which is sponsored or funded by an external body often has some form of evaluative process built in as part of the contract. It cannot be assumed that this will provide the information which the library taking part would wish to collect. The performance indicators commonly asked for sometimes have little relevance to the quality of service provision.

5.5 There is also a risk of bias in evaluation being undertaken by those people devising and running the training, partly because objectivity is difficult, and also because they may have a vested interest in the activity continuing.

5.6 A further decision which needs to be made is what information is to be collected. The issues of both the level of evaluation and when it is appropriate to evaluate were discussed in Chapter 4.

5.7 The information needed and the way it is collected will vary depending upon which level of evaluation is being undertaken.

5.7.1 Assessment of reactions, attitudes and learning will concentrate upon responses directly from those taking part, though some observation, peer evaluation and testing may be included.

5.7.2 Evaluation of effects on job behaviour will involve mostly testing and observation, but the perceptions and responses of participants will also be helpful.

5.7.3 At the level of assessment of organizational change, external measures which go beyond the responses, testing or observation of individuals need to be used, i.e. measures which concentrate upon processes and outputs of the library. These will include some elements of observation and testing of participants, but will also include reference to the performance indicators which are drawn from organizational objectives. For example, if the objective is to provide a cost-effective loan service, then efficiency measures such as cost per loan can be applied. In this case the aim of evaluation would be to establish a causal link between training activity and changes in the cost-effectiveness of the service.

5.8 The decision on when and whether to evaluate depends on the importance and expense of the activity, the frequency with which it is likely to be repeated, and the expense and difficulty of undertaking the evaluation.

5.8.1 *Importance*: If the training is for a large number of staff, or for a key task such as the implementation of an automated system, then it merits evaluation more than an individual attending an exhibition.

5.8.2 *Frequency*: If an activity is to be repeated, such as induction training, it is important to ensure that it is appropriate to the purpose and effective.

5.8.3 *Expense*: Sponsoring a member of staff on a higher degree will involve a much larger investment than sending staff to local professional meetings. This should be reflected in the effort to evaluate the activity.

5.9 The decision on what kind of evaluation to carry out will be influenced by the resources available for the purpose. As a general rule evaluative measures should be as simple and economical as possible. Resources are wasted if data are collected which are not needed. In addition, staff are more likely to respond to measures which do not take up too much time, and which they perceive to be relevant. Information should be collected only if there is an intention of following it up and taking appropriate action. Staff quickly lose confidence in procedures when they perceive that they are wasting their time completing forms and writing reports.

5.10 It is important that the evaluative process when started is completed, and any data collection is acted upon. Participants will quickly recognize the times when filling in questionnaires is a pointless activity, and will stop doing so if they feel they are wasting their effort.

5.11 To some extent the evaluative approach taken depends upon the original objective which is being addressed. If the training activity is to meet an immediate local need, perhaps an issue relating to an individual member of staff, evaluation should concentrate on reactions, learning and job behaviour. If, however, the activity is to meet a wider objective, such as the implementation of a new system, then evaluation of organizational change and job behaviour will probably be of greater importance. Thus, the evaluation of training should include the collection of information which will allow an assessment of whether the original objective has been achieved.

5.12 Although the decision on whether to evaluate and what information to collect will depend upon the activity being assessed there is a benefit in using some measures which are constant, irrespective of the activity. There is a danger that evaluative measures designed for a specific activity will share the values which underlie that activity. One of the key parts of the training cycle is to re-examine the original objectives and amend these if they appear subsequently to be inappropriate. The approach to collecting information for evaluation should be open enough to allow for this possibility. Additionally, even if the activity is fulfilling its objective, managers will need to know if it is also having some unforeseen and unintended consequences. An appropriately structured scheme of staff development or appraisal interviewing will be valuable for providing this kind of information.

5.13 When collecting information for evaluation there are a number of issues to be considered in ensuring that the data collected are reliable and valid. The validity of the information depends upon it relating to the questions which it will be used to answer. Collecting opinions of participants will be more valid for assessing attitude change than for measuring organizational change. Conversely, measuring changes in levels of efficiency will assess organizational change, but may not necessarily indicate changes in attitude or skills if other factors prevent these changes being translated into desired activity.

5.14 The reliability of an evaluative measure is the degree to which it comes up with a consistent and repeatable result. There are two aspects to this. The first is whether the information collected is consistent. For example, do participants respond differently to the same questionnaire if it is administered immediately following an activity or one month afterwards? The second aspect of reliability is whether the results can be unambiguously interpreted. If different assessors draw different conclusions from the same data then the results are less reliable. Alternatively, supervisors assessing the performance of tasks may allow personal opinions to affect their observations of different individuals. Training is a human activity, and there will always be elements of unreliability in its evaluation. Any measures used should recognize this and their design should be as value-free as possible. Sometimes the use of unreliable data is unavoidable, for example opinions of the quality of a trainer. When this is the case then the more responses are obtained from different individuals, the higher will be the reliability of the results.

6 Methods of collecting information

6.1 As discussed in Chapter 5, the approach taken to the evaluation of training should depend upon the activity itself, its general importance, its expense, how often it will be repeated and so on. There is a variety of techniques and tools for collecting information including checklists, questionnaires, reports, formal and informal interviews, observation, skills testing and measurement of organizational activity through general evaluation and the application of performance indicators. The use of financial measures, or activities described in these terms, as measures of cost-effectiveness and the use of performance indicators will be considered in the next two chapters.

6.2 *Checklists.* Checklists itemizing discrete activities which should have taken place can be used at either individual or organizational level. They might include a list of activities which need to be covered within a training programme, such as the elements which a new member of staff needs to know to be able to work without supervision at an issue point. Alternatively, for a training programme relating to a new procedure or system, a checklist might include all those members of staff who need to be trained. Checklists are not evaluative in the sense that they do not assess the quality of a training activity and do not refer to outcomes. They are useful as basic indications of whether intended activities have taken place, and may be part of the process of interviewing or of observation.

6.3 *Questionnaires.* Probably the examples of evaluation of training in practice most commonly found are questionnaires, particularly those which are distributed either at some stage during or after a training activity. They can be used, amongst other things, for gathering information about general needs for training and for attitudes to or perceptions of programmes of training. They will tend to be of most use in evaluating reactions to training and attitudes. A number of examples of these are included as appendices. There are several matters to consider in the use of questionnaires including what type of questions are to be asked, when the questionnaire should be distributed, if it should be repeated, how it is to be collected, and who should administer it.

6.3.1 There are various types of question and the choice of those used should relate to the information which is needed. In all cases the questions asked should be unambiguous, as misinterpretation by respondents will invalidate the results.

6.3.2 Open-ended questions followed by a blank for the response are useful for assessing opinions and attitudes. For example: 'What is your opinion of the quality of a training event?'

They are likely to lead to relatively long responses requiring more time in analysis than closed questions. If open-ended questions are being asked of a number of respondents it will be useful when analysing them to categorize the responses, even if account is being taken of the individual opinions expressed.

6.3.3 Closed questions give respondents a choice of predetermined answers. They range from (1) giving two choices of response through (2) multiple choice to (3) checklists. Examples of questions in these forms are:

(1) The training activity met the objectives outlined at the beginning of the session:

      YES   NO   (tick one)

(2) Rate the quality of the learning materials on a scale of 1 (excellent) to 5 (terrible)

      1   2   3   4   5

(3) Why did you attend this training activity? (tick those which are appropriate)

      Personal interest
      It is part of a programme
      Colleagues were already attending
      Instructed to by a supervisor
      It is a requirement of the job
      etc.

6.3.4 Closed questions are easier to analyse than open-ended questions, but it is essential to ensure that the possible answers allow respondents to say what they feel. Closed questions may be combined with open-ended questions which ask for an expansion of the answer, and checklists in particular may include a final choice of 'other (please specify)'. The scales on multiple-choice questions need to be considered carefully, and some questionnaires give these as a series of faces looking more or less 'smiley' or glum. It is sometimes thought that with an odd number of possible answers to multiple-choice questions (i.e. three or five) respondents will tend to give the average or middle response. If this is likely they should be given an even number of choices which will force them to make a qualitative judgement of some sort. If several multiple-choice questions are asked the scales should run in the same direction. That is, if one represents the worst possible evaluation for the first question asked, it should do so for all subsequent questions. In addition, some questions may need a 'no opinion/not relevant' response.

6.3.5 If questionnaires are to be distributed on a wide scale it may be appropriate to use some form of automation to collate the results. Certain forms of layout facilitate the input of data through a keyboard. There are software tools available which automatically lay out questions within fixed formats and subsequently produce analyses of the results from input data.

6.3.6 Questionnaires asking participants to assess the content and quality of training events need particular consideration. These are usually distributed at the end of a training event, often as part of the final session. This may not always be the most effective way to use them. Participants may feel particularly positive at the time if, for example, working in groups has formed strong working relationships with fellow participants, or pleasant surroundings have removed some of the daily pressures of the working environment. After a period of reflection this positive 'glow' may fade, and the event can be assessed in a more objective way. Some organizations ask participants to complete two questionnaires, one at the end of an event, and the second some weeks afterwards. This allows the first to assess immediate reactions to the input to the training – the quality of the trainers, the learning materials, the surroundings, for example – and the second to comment on the value of the training and its likely outcome in terms of changes in practice. However, participants may be reluctant to spend time completing subsequent questionnaires, and the response rate to these can be low. Distributing two questionnaires also requires more resources. Unless circumstances dictate otherwise it may be appropriate to circulate only one questionnaire, and accept that the responses will necessarily be subjective.

6.3.7 If the training is part of a continuing process over a period of time then it will be worth carrying out evaluation with brief questionnaires as the programme progresses. This enables immediate responses to trainers, and the training environment to be responded to more quickly.

6.3.8 Responses to questionnaires may be affected by who distributes and collects them. If responses have to be returned to the person who delivered the training, then participants may be reluctant to be critical. This may be overcome by having them distributed and collected by an independent person such as the training officer. However, the response rate will probably fall unless they are collected immediately. Allowing responses to be anonymous can improve the response rate if participants find it difficult to criticize, whether questionnaires are collected immediately or at a later date. Allowing anonymity means that the responses cannot be used to relate training more closely to individual needs, though, where, for example, different members of staff respond in varying ways to specific forms of training. Levels of satisfaction with a training event may reflect the needs of the individual as much as the content of the training.

6.3.9 It is important that response rates to questionnaires, and indeed any evaluation which is undertaken, are as high as possible. The administration of the evaluation can contribute to a high response rate by making clear the deadline for the completion of forms, and where they need to be returned. Response rates may be increased by strategies such as asking for evaluation forms to be returned with expenses claims. It is important that evaluation is seen at all levels to be a fundamental part of the training process. Completing questionnaires or other evaluation should not be seen as an optional extra. Some organizations try to require that evaluation of training, in whatever form that may take, is automatically undertaken, though ensuring that this takes place is difficult in practice. Making completion of questionnaires mandatory risks giving the impression that the activity is onerous. As in all of the other areas considered, the effort put into achieving high response rates depends on the importance and details of the event being assessed.

6.3.10 The use of questionnaires is therefore surrounded with potential difficulties. Information acquired with open-ended questions is likely to be of more use, but will also be more difficult to analyse than answers to closed questions. Allowing participants time to reflect on their experience will give greater objectivity, but may reduce response rates. Respondents may feel anonymity allows them to express their views more freely, but it might also limit the use of the information gained. Decisions on all these issues will be a compromise depending upon the use to which the information will be put.

6.4 *Reports.* Another method of ascertaining personal responses to training is to ask for written reports to be produced. These may run to a prescribed format asking for information on the content and quality of the training, the response of the participant, and the likely outcomes in terms of organizational change. Alternatively they may be open to allow for a wide variety of forms of training to be reported upon. These take more time for the respondent to complete than questionnaires, and they are likely to take more time to analyse.

6.4.1 Reports are likely to be useful for a new or developing activity, and more appropriate where a programme of activity requires a large input of resources. It is also more feasible to use written reports as an evaluative technique where the numbers participating are limited. Respondents may be more reluctant to write reports than they are to complete questionnaires due to the greater amount of time required. Though still concentrating upon individual reactions to training, written reports by their nature allow for more reflection upon the activity being evaluated and consideration of changes in individual behaviour than do questionnaires.

6.4.2 As with questionnaires, if reports are needed they should be treated by the organization as essential and not optional. It is again important that the organization responds to the information contained in reports, otherwise participants will see them as a pointless exercise.

6.4.3 When an activity is unique, or has required a high input of resources, it may be appropriate to require a verbal report as a presentation to a group, rather than a written account. These will typically involve the respondent in sharing information acquired in an activity, but should also include some attempt to assess the importance and quality of the activity itself.

6.5 *Interviews.* Interviews can be used to ascertain all of the information obtained in questionnaires and reports, but also allow elucidation of the responses.

6.5.1 The most common use of interviewing as a way of evaluating training will be as part of the cycle defining and meeting staff development needs, and may be subsumed as part of a more general appraisal process. In this case interviews will take place on a regular basis. As with written reports, they are better if they run to a particular format with a list of issues to be covered. The individual can be asked to complete a preliminary form beforehand which then becomes part of the basis for the discussion. After the discussion has taken place a further document should be produced, again within a fixed format, which details important points from the interview and highlights future actions which need to be taken. Both participants in the interview should be given the chance to agree that it reflects accurately the discussion which took place. The report itself can then be used as part of the general process of evaluating the appropriateness of training, its quality and relevance as well as contributing to the formulation of future training plans. The report should also form part of the input of subsequent interviews where the extent and effectiveness with which the actions highlighted have taken place can be assessed.

6.5.2   Interviews typically take place between individuals and their line manager, or sometimes involve the training officer. As with questionnaires the person undertaking the interviewing may affect the responses. If the interviewer has undertaken some of the training then the participant may be reluctant to be critical of its content or execution. It is important that the interviewer is not threatening, and understands the perspective of the interviewee.

6.5.3   For new or developing activities, and those which have required a large input of resources, it may be appropriate to interview staff outside the normal staff development/appraisal interviewing cycle. Again, the interview should result in a report to which the participants both agree. Interviews are resource-intensive, taking up the time of the participants at the interview, the preparation for the interview, and production of the report. The decision on whether to undertake interviews should be based on the importance of the information which is going to be obtained.

6.5.4   Interviews allow for evaluation of reactions and attitudes. They also give some scope for assessing any individual behavioural change, and to some extent allow for discussion at the level of organizational change.

6.6   *Testing.* An assessment of whether skills, attitudes or knowledge have been acquired can be made with the use of tests. There is a huge literature relating to testing, and the subject continues to be a matter of debate in academic circles. The reader can follow up the discussions elsewhere, while this Training Guide will focus on the particular aspects of testing which relate to the evaluation of training.

6.6.1   During or after a particular training activity has taken place participants can be tested to see whether:

- they have understood what was intended
- they have learned new information
- they can put this understanding or knowledge to practical use
- they have acquired a practical skill
- they have changed their attitudes

6.6.2   Testing is more accurate and reliable when it focuses on the acquisition of knowledge and practical skills such as knowledge of reference sources or ability to use computers to undertake given activities. It is less reliable where it examines attitudes. For example, participants may recognize that they are expected to display particular attitudes after a training activity relating to equal opportunities issues, and respond appropriately to questions even if they do not share those attitudes.

6.6.3   It cannot be assumed that acquired skills or knowledge will necessarily be translated into workplace behaviour. Staff may understand the important elements of customer care, but still not put them into practice. If this needs to be taken into account the testing should be undertaken in the work environment.

6.6.4 Results from testing will indicate whether learning, or the acquisition of skills, has taken place. It may not show exactly why training has or has not succeeded. Explanations for training not being successful include inappropriate training techniques being used, the wrong staff being trained, peer-group pressures, and inadequate preparation on the part of the organization or the individuals concerned. Clarifying connections like these will need a combination of evaluative measures, for example testing and interviews together.

6.6.5 Tests can take a variety of forms. They may require written responses to questions. As with questionnaires these can be closed or open-ended, and many of the comments made in Section 6.3 apply equally to testing. Open-ended questions allow respondents to be more expansive, but the responses to them are more difficult to evaluate unless there is a simple, clearly correct answer. Closed questions may ask for a choice to be made between two answers, for example YES/NO, or be multiple choice asking the respondent to pick the correct or most appropriate answer from a list.

6.6.6 Testing may also involve requiring staff to demonstrate a skill such as operating a piece of equipment or working at an issue point. The result will be important, but often the process may need to be observed to know whether it is being undertaken properly, and if not, why not. For example, a test may involve looking at whether an individual can load paper in a photocopier. Where the skill being tested is more general, such as dealing with users, then the role of the observer is not so clearly defined. Observation as a means of evaluation will be discussed more fully in Section 6.7, but observation as a method of testing skills needs to be carried out within clearly defined parameters. The observer should have a checklist of appropriate activity or expected behaviour. This will minimize the risk of the evaluation being subjective. Staff undertaking evaluation also need to be trained to perform the role in an objective and unthreatening manner.

6.6.7 Adults at work are often uncomfortable about being tested, partly because they may feel it is a process to which only schoolchildren are subjected, and therefore demeaning. They may also be concerned that testing is an assessment of them personally, rather than an evaluation of the training process. These fears can partly be met by making the reason for undertaking the testing clear. In addition, there are also ways of reducing the stress on the individuals involved in testing. Computers can be used to record and evaluate responses, and many computer-assisted learning (CAL) packages have this facility built in. If the training being evaluated involves use of an automated system it may well be possible to use the computer to test skill and learning unobtrusively. Similarly, if the member of staff is being tested for their ability to undertake a process they may feel under less pressure if they are recorded using a discreet video camera rather than being watched directly by another individual.

6.6.8 There are many potential pitfalls in using testing as a means of evaluation.

It is at its least contentious when assessing learning of defined skills and knowledge. Even here testing of individuals should be handled with discretion. If there is a need to test understanding or attitudes then particular guidance should be sought from the literature or experts in the field. Testing as a means of evaluating training also needs to be undertaken in conjunction with other forms of assessment. Testing will establish whether there has been a transfer of knowledge, skills or attitudes; the other forms of evaluation will indicate why particular results have been obtained.

6.7 *Observation.* Processes can be evaluated by observing them taking place. In the evaluation of training this can be of use in two main areas. The first of these is observing what is taking place during a training activity. The second is to assess the behaviour of employees at work, and their ability to undertake given functions.

6.7.1 Observation needs to be approached with caution. It was noted in Section 4.14 that the fact of being observed can alter the behaviour of the staff being watched. This may be because they are responding to an interest being shown in their activity. Alternatively, staff may know what behaviour is expected of them, but unless they actually accept that it is appropriate they may act in that way only when they are being watched.

6.7.2 It may be better to adopt some methods of unobtrusive observation. Video-recording of activity, especially if it takes place over time, may reduce pressure on the staff being observed, particularly when they get accustomed to the presence of a camera. This can also be a more economical use of staff time as an observer may have to spend a great deal of time before the staff involved feel comfortable and begin to act normally. There is a risk of creating a feeling of a 'Big Brother' approach, and this technique should be used only with the full knowledge and consent of the staff involved.

6.7.3 Alternatively, observation may be carried out by staff who are familiar and would normally be expected to be present in a particular environment. The supervisor or line manager in a section should in any case be aware of the activities taking place within their area. They will need training to be able to observe and report back on behaviour in a supportive and objective way. They may need a checklist of activities which they should be observing.

6.7.4 A recent development is the concept of peer evaluation. In this case staff who are undertaking the same or similar roles as a group observe themselves and report on the activities taking place. This needs to be managed carefully so that it is a supportive process, and does not take place in an atmosphere of competition or suspicion. The group should meet and, in conjunction with the line managers and training officer, agree on the objectives and activities with which they are concerned. They should also be given training in observing activities and reporting back in a constructive and supportive way. The group can then provide feedback into the training cycle about needs for training, and how far training is being effective.

6.7.5 Observation can also be a tool for assessing the effectiveness of a trainer or method of training by watching the activity taking place. This is a technique which is a normal part of teacher training. It needs to be undertaken by persons who are themselves skilled trainers or lecturers. Observers in this situation will normally work with a checklist relating to the style and pace of the trainer, the quality and content of the training materials, the layout of the room, the use of audiovisual aids and so on. They should provide feedback to the trainer as appropriate. The issue of evaluating training provided by external agents will be dealt with in Chapter 9.

6.7.6 Observation is a time-consuming process, and therefore expensive in the use of resources. In most cases it is more appropriate to the assessment of behavioural change of individuals and organizational change within particular sections. Observation as a technique of evaluation should be used carefully to avoid being threatening to the staff involved. At all stages it should be clear that it is part of the wider process of the training cycle.

6.8 There is thus a variety of techniques which can be used to gather information about the effectiveness of training. The processes used will reflect the information which is required, and the importance of the activity being assessed should dictate the resources which will be available to evaluate any particular activity. The techniques described in this chapter cover the levels of individual change and to some extent organizational change. The next chapter will concentrate on methods of assessing whether change has taken place on a wider organizational level.

 # Cost-effectiveness and return on investment

7.1 From the general literature of the evaluation of training it would appear that measurements of cost-effectiveness and return on investment are common in commercial environments. Library and information services in organizations which regularly use financial measures as yardsticks of success will be in a better position to apply these to the evaluation of training than those in the public sector. However, with the growth of privatization and other changes in the political environment, libraries in the public sector are increasingly taking a commercial approach to the delivery of services. There will always be parts of public service provision which, except in the broadest terms, cannot be defined in terms of financial value, but it is worth examining the general approach to be able to make use of concepts of cost-effectiveness where they are appropriate.

7.2 Cost-effectiveness is a very simple idea. All of the costs of undertaking an activity are added together. These are then compared to the results of the activity either as financial savings or as increased productivity and efficiency expressed in financial terms. The greater the ratio of savings or increased productivity compared to the original investment in undertaking the activity, the greater the cost-effectiveness of the activity. If the resultant savings are less than the original investment then the activity was not cost-effective. The financial value of any increased productivity resulting from an activity compared to the costs of producing that increase is sometimes referred to as the 'return on investment'.

7.3 The difficulty with adopting this approach to library provision is assigning financial values to service outputs which are socially or culturally defined, though this is not always impossible. Many of the processes which lead to the provision of library services can be and already are measured in financial terms. For example, cost will clearly be a major factor in deciding whether to have library materials serviced by suppliers, or in-house. Taking this example further, another factor in such a decision will be the speed with which materials are supplied serviced and unserviced. Even if there is a great cost saving in having materials supplied already serviced, if the speed of supply is slowed to an unacceptable point then the decision may be taken to have unserviced materials supplied. In this case the speed of supply will effectively have been given a value, i.e. the point at which the additional length of time taken to deliver the materials outweighed the cost savings. Thus, whether consciously or not, library managers will often assign financial values to activities which do not in themselves have a cost or price.

7.4 There are a number of general areas which can be considered in the measurement of the cost-effectiveness of training in libraries and information services. These include the following:

7.4.1   *Time savings.* These occur where the training results in staff having to spend less time in producing an undiminished product or service, or where a process is undertaken with less staff time than previously. An example might be where meetings take less time to reach acceptable and appropriate decisions after the chair has undertaken a staff development activity on the efficient management of meetings.

7.4.2   *Reduction in training costs.* This applies specifically to staff development programmes. In this case the organizational objective is achieved by methods which are less expensive when measured in the costs of staff time, travelling and the training itself. For example, running a course for ten people in-house may prove to be cheaper than sending those staff away to be trained when all of the costs involved are included. Alternatively, an open learning course might produce considerable savings if the alternative is sending staff a long distance for their training. In terms of cost-effectiveness, activities which produce reductions in training costs should be seen to be producing the same results. If the new activity is not as effective in meeting the training needs then it is not necessarily more cost-effective.

7.4.3   *Improved use of materials.* This includes training which leads to staff being more efficient in their use of materials, or which results in less waste of materials through mistakes. Examples might include savings in paper when printers are loaded more efficiently, or less waste when expensive multi-part forms are completed correctly first time.

7.4.4   *Avoiding correction or supervision.* There is an expense in checking for and recovering mistakes, for example in the class numbers assigned to books or on the spine labels attached to them. Training which enables staff to be more accurate, and reduces the time which has to be spent in checking or subsequently retrieving mistakes, cuts this expense.

7.5   There are other areas which might be suitable for a cost-benefit approach to training in a more commercial environment. These include the following:

7.5.1   *Penalty avoidance.* This is where there is a financial incentive to produce a service or product to a deadline. Training which enables these deadlines to be met can be justified in terms of the likely cost saving.

7.5.2   *Savings on liability.* If the organization is legally responsible for the accuracy of the information it supplies there could be a cost justification for training in savings of potential costs and legal expenses.

7.5.3   *Opportunities for profit.* If information services are charged for *pro rata*, according to the amount of information or number of documents supplied, then reducing the time spent in delivering each item offers the opportunity to deliver and charge for more items in a given time.

7.6   There are also areas where there may well be an identifiable benefit from training, but expressing this benefit in cost terms will be difficult. These include targets such as producing a better service, raising levels of user satisfaction, and raising staff morale. These may be measurable on some scale even if it is not expressed in financial terms. Chapter 8 will look at ways of measuring organizational change in more non-financial terms.

7.7 It is worth considering a detailed example of how a cost-effectiveness calculation would work. To do this the example given in 7.4.1 will be expanded. This looks at the savings which can be made by running meetings more efficiently, and sets it against the costs of giving the person who takes the chair training in managing meetings.

7.8 Suppose a team with eight members has a weekly meeting which lasts for an average of 1.5 hours. Some of the team need to travel to the meeting, at a cost of £15.00 each week in travelling expenses. The weekly cost of the meeting will be the hourly wages (say an average of £12.00 per hour) multiplied by the length of the meeting, plus the travelling expenses. The annual cost is this figure multiplied by the number of meetings each year (say 48, allowing for holidays). The cost of the meetings each year will therefore be:

Weekly wages: 1.5 x 8 x £12.00	= £144.00
Travelling expenses	= £ 15.00
Weekly total	= £159.00

ANNUAL TOTAL = £159.00 x 48 = £7,632.00

The cost of sending the person who takes the chair on a training activity will be the cost of the event, plus travelling expenses, plus the cost of the wages for the period of absence (say 8 hours at £16.00 per hour):

Cost of one training day	£150.00
Travelling & subsistence	£ 40.00
Wages cost 8 x £16.00	£128.00

TOTAL COST OF TRAINING £318.00

For this example we will suppose that the training was successful, and the average length of the meetings was reduced by 30 minutes to 1 hour. The annual cost of the meetings would subsequently be:

Weekly wages: 1 x 8 x £12.00	= £ 96.00
Travelling expenses	= £ 15.00
Weekly total	= £111.00

ANNUAL TOTAL = £111.00 x 48 = £5,328.00

The savings made would therefore be £7,632 - £5,328 = £2304.00. When this is set against the training costs of £318.00 there is a clear cost-benefit of having the member of staff attend the training course. In this example the meetings would have to be shortened by an average of less than six minutes each to reach the break-even point of paying back the original investment in training.

7.9 This is a simple example. In practice it will not usually be so easy to identify and quantify the benefits deriving from specific training activities. In the first place the link between the activity and the desired outcome may not be so direct. In addition, as outlined in Section 4.14, besides the effects of any training, there could well be other factors influencing individual and organizational behaviour. There are also some aspects of library service which cannot be reduced to financial equivalents. However, cost-benefit approaches to training in libraries can be useful so long as the limitations are borne in mind.

7.10   The cost-benefit approach can be useful because it provides a tool which allows a more objective analysis of activities. It can also focus on the real costs of providing services. Library and information services are often labour-intensive, and it is often too easy to ignore the real costs, including salaries, of service provision. Where a calculation involves a major element of staff time it should be remembered that the costs of employing staff are higher than the hourly salary which they are paid. Organizations now routinely add a figure for 'on-costs' to salaries to arrive at the true cost of employing a person. On-costs cover insurance, pensions and other payments which the employer must make, and may add more than 10% to staff costs.

7.11   The above example refers only to time savings, but similar calculations could be made looking at reductions in training costs, improved use of materials, the avoidance of correction or supervision or any of the more commercial aspects mentioned in Section 7.5.

7.12   Apart from evaluation during and after an event, managers of library services might well find analysis in terms of finance useful when justifying an activity which is proposed. Taking the example in 7.8, it might, at the outset, appear difficult to justify expenditure in real terms of over £300 on a one-day training activity. When that cost is set in the context of the consequent expected savings then the expenditure becomes much more reasonable. In addition, having argued the case for the activity on the basis of cost-effectiveness, there is a ready-made measure for assessing whether the activity has achieved its objective.

 # Evaluation and performance indicators

8.1 Chapter 7 looked at cost-benefit as an approach to the evaluation of training. This is a tool which is apparently used more frequently in commercial environments than in library services. The reasons for its lack of use in libraries may be cultural differences amongst the managers, or just reluctance to try new methods. There are, though, also some elements of library provision which cannot be measured in financial terms. This has long been recognized, and managers of libraries should be familiar with the evaluations of library services in general which try to assess library activities. More recently performance indicators have been used as an audit approach to public service provision, and although these tend to be quantitative rather than a measure of the quality of services they do provide measures of outcomes against which training might be evaluated.

8.2 As with cost-benefit analysis the use of evaluative measures of library activity, and particularly performance indicators, to assess the effects of training must be approached with caution. The same drawbacks apply in establishing a firm causal link between any training activity and the organizational outcome. Any changes in organizational behaviour are likely to have been influenced by a whole range of different factors. Nevertheless, evaluation and performance indicators can provide information about organizational behaviour in the ways that the methods described in Chapter 6 can provide information about individual attitudes, learning and activity.

8.3 Out of the range of possible library activities which can be evaluated, the ones of interest here are those which concern organizational change as an outcome of training and staff development. These will vary depending upon the objective which the training is intended to achieve, but they might include the following:

8.3.1 *Attitude changes*, such as raising staff morale, or improving user perceptions of services.

8.3.2 *Behaviour changes*, such as increasing participation rates in a population of potential users or extending the types of service of which particular groups make use.

8.3.3 *Organizational changes*, which can be measured but not assigned a financial value, such as increasing issues of stock, or the length of time taken to retrieve information from a system.

8.4 There are several sources where more information can be found on the evaluation of library services, and there is no point in giving great detail here. Chapter 2 covered the general points to be considered in evaluation.

These are that qualitative data are usually more useful than quantitative, but generally more difficult to obtain; that evaluative measures should be relative to give them meaning; that quality is not an absolute measure, but itself is relative to demands or needs; and that evaluation is undertaken for one or more of a variety of reasons, and the approach taken may vary according to the need for the information.

8.5 Evaluation of a library or information service will involve some combination of a quantification of activity in financial or numerical terms, and an assessment of attitudes, opinions and values of users, members of staff and other significant groups in the organizational environment. Many of the techniques described in Chapter 6 can equally well be used for gathering more general information on these groups. Surveys of opinions and use, observation and interviewing can all obtain useful information about perceptions of, attitudes to and needs for services, and changes in behaviour. Surveys of library users are common. Surveys of non-users are less common, but likely to provide useful information.

8.6 For the evaluation of training these methods are probably of most use in providing data over a period of time. For example, if the objective of a training activity was to improve customer care at an issue point, then a survey of the perceptions of users before and after the training will give an indication of the effectiveness of the training. Of course, the manager needs to be aware of the other factors in the environment described in Section 4.14 which might also affect behaviour, and user perceptions of it.

8.7 Surveys, interviewing and observation will also be useful in a situation where the characteristics of the population are unknown. Libraries collect some information about their users during a registration process, but if an objective is set which defines users in terms other than those described by the existing data then the information will have to be obtained by other means. For example, if it is hoped that an activity will lead to increased use of services by a particular group of users defined by age or social background, it may be necessary to survey these groups. Alternatively, the expected outcome of training may relate to people who use a service, but do not register as users.

8.8 Organizations routinely collect data which provide information on organizational change. The financial details from the accounting systems are one source, but libraries, as any other bureaucratic organization, are constantly counting and measuring. Details commonly collected include issue statistics, numbers of enquiries, numbers of registered users, numbers of staff, and their gradings, details of accommodation, numbers of user spaces, opening hours, and so on.

8.9 These figures in themselves are usually meaningless. Issue statistics will be a measure of how much clerical work is needed to charge out materials, discharge them and return them to the shelves, but they give little information about the value of the issues to the individual users, to users as a whole, or to the organization. Relative measures such as issues per user, issues per member of staff, issues per item in stock, or cost per issue give a much better starting point for use in evaluation. These are the kinds of measure which are used as performance indicators, and they are open to criticism that as quantitative measures they do not actually evaluate activity. The examples given, for instance, would not give any indication of what kind of use has been made of the materials borrowed. However, they are much more likely to provide information relevant to measuring organizational change. A library will probably not have 'increase issues' as an objective, but 'increase issues per head of population' and particularly 'decrease cost per issue' are much more likely to form the basis of library planning.

8.10 The performance indicator type of information becomes much more useful when it is combined with the other more qualitative data which can be acquired. To continue the use of issue statistics as an example, increased loans per user do not necessarily give an indication of user satisfaction with the service. If, however, they are combined over a period of time with the results of surveys of user opinions, then the conclusion which can be drawn is much clearer.

8.11 The collection of information in itself is a pointless activity. Its use is in describing whether organizational objectives have been achieved. A library therefore needs to describe its objectives in measurable outcomes, and then collect the information which indicates whether these have been achieved. The information collected to evaluate training is only a part of this wider perspective.

8.12 As with the evaluation of training, more general evaluation of services can be expensive and difficult. Unless the training is a major activity then it will not be justified to go to great expense in acquiring the information. Libraries should, though, be evaluating their services over time, and much of the information and analysis will prove relevant to the specific evaluation of training. The evaluation should be based upon identifiable outcomes which are drawn directly from the objectives of the library mission statement. These may be qualitative, such as 'improve customer perceptions', quantitative, such as 'reduce the average time taken to satisfy reservations', or financial, such as 'reduce the cost per issue'.

9 Training provided by external agents

9.1 The discussion so far has considered general matters to do with the evaluation of training. Training provided by external agents is worth particular attention. Activity which comes in this area ranges through the purchase of training materials of various types, sending staff to training events and conferences, having consultants deliver an agreed programme either at the location of the library or at an external location, or having staff complete a longer-term course, often leading to the award of a qualification.

9.2 The approaches to evaluation already described will be applicable. Whether the training is in-house or provided externally, the process of choosing the activity based on organizational objectives and perceived needs, monitoring the activity, and then assessing the outcome and revising either the programme or the objectives will be the same. However, there are some additional factors to be considered. First, the client organization will usually have less control over the training activity, so it is important to ensure that the content and approach are appropriate, and that the quality of what is actually delivered is as expected. Also, the prospective deliverer of the training activity may be unknown to the client organization. Care needs to be taken that the expense of training is not wasted.

9.3 Many of the activities which come into this area are difficult to evaluate because the benefits are going to be relatively intangible. External courses and conferences are often valuable because they allow staff to establish contact with others who share their interests. This is particularly useful for those who work in small organizations. The value of this contact will vary depending upon the other individuals who attend the activity, and the needs of the member of staff at that time, and so formally evaluating the outcome in these terms will often be impossible.

9.4 Training provided by external agents can be divided into two main types: either ready-made packages and events, or activities which are designed to fit the needs of the client organization.

9.5 Packages which are bought in include everything from stand-alone training materials in printed, audiovisual or computer form, to external events such as conferences, exhibitions and short courses, and longer courses. All of the evaluative measures discussed so far can be used.

9.6 If possible, it is worth previewing learning materials before they are purchased. This is particularly the case where the materials are expensive, such as some of the videos and computer-assisted learning programmes which are available. Judgements need to be made about the approach and level as well as the content of the materials. They may be needed to fulfil a particular purpose, but it is also worth considering whether they will be of more lasting use.

9.7 When arranging training which has to be delivered by external staff it is important that the organization continues to carry out its own evaluation, and does not rely on that undertaken by the external provider. As with the evaluation of training in general the results of the evaluation of external provision should be acted on. If the outcome of sending staff to a training event is not what had been expected because of the quality of the event, or because the objectives outlined by the external provider were not kept to, then the client organization should seriously consider not sending any more staff. If the external organization is associated with a professional body, or part of a cooperative approach to the provision of training then the results of the evaluation should be shared with the wider group.

9.8 When training is being delivered by an external body, but it is designed to meet the specific needs of the organization then there are a number of further points which should be considered. In this case there should be initial contacts and discussion with the provider prior to the event, the delivery of the training and then reporting back as a follow-up activity.

9.9 When initial discussions are held the external agents should make efforts to understand and respond to the needs of the organization. If they prefer to concentrate on their own approach or product then the commissioning agents should be wary. External providers should produce a clear outline of what will be delivered, how it will be approached, and the expected outcomes. It is important for the client organization to be clear about its own needs at this stage.

9.10 The delivery of external courses should also be monitored closely. They should be well prepared, with good-quality training materials. The organization of the event itself is important, and trainers should have any necessary equipment and accommodation needs arranged beforehand. The delivery itself should be evaluated either with questionnaires to participants or by observation of the activity itself.

9.11 The follow-up to an activity is important. The external body should report back its perception of outcomes and how these should be responded to. They are almost certain to have evaluated the activity, and hopefully they will share this with the client organization.

9.12 The techniques of evaluation of training provided by external agents are therefore no different to those for evaluating training in general, though more emphasis may be needed on assessing quality and content before the event or the purchase of materials. However, as external training is likely to be both expensive and less within the control of the client organization, then it is crucial that evaluation is undertaken.

10 Evaluation checklist

For the process of the evaluation of training the following points need to be considered.

1   Assess the need for training, for both the organization and the individual, and arrive at a continuing plan with clear objectives.

2   Design and deliver the training and staff development, being clear about the intended outcomes. Make sure participants in the training understand and agree with those intended outcomes.

3   Measure the outcomes of the training at the levels of the reactions of the individuals involved, what they have learned, whether this has changed their behaviour, and what changes in organizational activity have taken place.

4   Compare the demonstrated outcomes to the stated objectives. If there is a mismatch review the original objectives and/or the content and delivery of the training.

5   Revise the training plan in the light of the evaluation.

6   Use evaluation as appropriate to the activity being examined. The more important, expensive or frequently repeated the activity, the more justified is the investment in evaluation. Be clear about the real costs of training, including the time of the staff attending.

7   Do not waste time collecting information for evaluation unless you intend to use it and act upon it.

Bibliography

Bibliographic searches produce long lists of references on the subject of the evaluation of training, many of which are strong on theory. The items here will all be of practical use.

Books

Blanksby, Margaret, *Staff training, a librarians' handbook*, Newcastle under Lyme, Association of Assistant Librarians, 1988.
A general text on training which puts evaluation into its wider context.

Bramley, Peter, *Evaluation of training, a practical guide*, Centre for Training and Evaluation Studies, Birkbeck College, 1986.
The best general guide to evaluation. If you read only one source it should be this one.

Edwards, Judith, *Evaluation in adult and further education, a practical handbook for teachers and organisers*, Liverpool, Workers Educational Association, 1991.
One example from many of a guide to the evaluation of education and learning. It also examines evaluation of wider aspects of process of delivery.

Employment Department, Further and Higher Education Branch, *Evaluation for learning*, Sheffield, The Department, 1993.
Two booklets in a folder which examine evaluation of learning and the delivery of education.

Hamblin, A. C., *Evaluation and control of training*, London, McGraw-Hill, 1974.
One of the large number of sources on the theoretical approaches to training. Not much has changed since 1974.

Phillips, Jack J., *Handbook of training and evaluation methods*, 2nd edn, London, Kogan Page, 1991.
An American text which provides a complete approach to evaluation. It concentrates on examples which might be considered appropriate in a commercial environment.

Sheal, Peter R., *How to develop and present staff training courses*, London, Kogan Page, 1989.
Although this examines a particular form of training it gives practical examples and puts evaluation into context.

Training & Development Lead Body, *National standards for training and development*, Sheffield, Employment Department, 1992.
The guidelines by which trainers themselves will be assessed.

Williamson, Michael G., *The evaluation of training* in *Handbook of library training practice*, vol.2 edited by Ray Prytherch, Aldershot, Gower, 1990. 226-62.
A good practical guide.

Periodical articles

Duncan, Mark, 'Evaluating training vendors', *Computer world*, 17 April 1989, 120.

A brief but useful guide to assessing training provided by external agents.

Endres, Garrett, 'How to measure management training and develop effectiveness', *Journal of European industrial training*, **14**(9), 1990, 3-7.

A realistic guide which highlights possible sources of bias.

Phillips, Jack J., 'Measuring the return on HRD', *Employment relations today*, **18**(3), Autumn 1991, 329-42.

This article focuses on the financial aspects of evaluating training.

Roberts, Alan, 'Evaluating training programmes', *International trade forum*, **26** (4), Oct./Dec. 1990, 18-23.

A basic introduction.

Smith, Alison, 'Evaluation of management training, subjectivity and the individual', *Journal of european training*, **14**(1), 1990, 12-15.

Highlights the weaknesses in evaluation sheets.

Spencer, Lyle M., 'How to calculate the costs and benefits of an HRD program', *Training*, Jul. 1984, 40–51.

A good exposition of the cost-benefit approach.

Appendix

The following forms are examples of evaluation which are actually in use. They illustrate some of the different approaches which can be taken.

Examples 1 and 2 are post-activity forms to assess the immediate reactions of participants. Form 1 in particular makes use of the well-loved 'smiley' faces.

Example 3 is a form to be used at some time after an activity has been completed, and the participant has had time to reflect on its relevance and effect. It includes a section for the comments of the line manager, and so goes beyond measuring participant reactions.

Example 4 is a form to assess participant opinions which consists entirely of open-ended questions.

Forms 5, 6 and 7 are for the evaluation of specific types of training materials. Example 7 refers to open learning materials which might well be complete activities in themselves.

Example 8 is for the evaluation of an externally provided activity by an observer rather than a participant.

Form 9 is used for evaluation of a lecturer by an observer.

Example 10 is an evaluation form used by an external course provider.

Examples 11 and 12 are forms to be used when undertaking annual staff development interviews. Form 11 is filled in before the interview, and 12 is the agreed result of discussions. They give the opportunity to comment on past staff development activities, and as part of the review in the following year also set those objectives which activities are intended to meet.

Example 1

NORFOLK COUNTY COUNCIL
COURSE EVALUATION FORM

tw form 10

We hope you found our Course of value. To assist in evaluating the effectiveness of the Course, would you please complete and return this form to the Course Administrator, Room 501, within one week of the Course completion.

COURSE TITLE: _____

VENUE: _____

NAME: _____ DEPT. _____

TEL.No. _____ DATE: _____

1. COURSE CONTENT

General content of course

Relevance of material covered

Amount of material covered

Was the course in line with your expectations?

Did you find the course informative?

What topics could be added or covered in more detail?

What topics could be omitted or covered in less detail?

What were the most relevant sessions of the course (for you)?

Was the course: Too Long ☐   Satisfactory Length ☐   Too Short ☐

Please continue overleaf

Example 1 continued

tw form 11

COURSE PRESENTATION

☺ ☺ ☺ ☹ ☹

Trainer delivery and instruction

Was the content presented in a well organised and clear way?

Were questions answered to everyone's satisfaction?

Quality of handouts / OHP's etc.

Other comments:

COURSE VENUE:

☺ ☺ ☺ ☹ ☹

Training room / Quality of accommodation

Seating

Meals

Other comments:

GENERAL

☺ ☺ ☺ ☹ ☹

Administration of the course

Pre-Course Information / Course programme

Other comments:

How would you rate the overall value of the course to your work?
VERY VALUABLE
VALUABLE
OF LITTLE VALUE
NO VALUE

THANKYOU FOR YOUR HELP.

Example 2

Suffolk County Council
Arts and Libraries Department

COURSE EVALUATION QUESTIONNAIRE

Name: ....

Post: ....

Course attended: ....

Venue: .... Date(s): ....

What were your reasons for attending the course?

Various aspects of the course are covered in the chart below. Please complete each section by placing a tick under the face which most resembles your own reaction. Please add any explanatory comments in the right hand column.

	😞	🙁	😐	🙂	😊	YOUR COMMENTS
Your general opinion of the course as a whole						
Did the course achieve its aims, as you understood them?						
To what extent were your aims in attending met?						
How do you feel about the length of the course?						
Were you happy about the subjects chosen for inclusion?						
Were you happy about the treatment of the subjects?						
Was the practical/ theoretical balance right?						
How did you feel about the intellectual level of the course?						
Were you happy about the facilities and arrangements?						

Example 2 continued

Please list in the left hand column the various sessions of the course and then mark out of 10 (top score 10, lowest 0) under each of the following aspects:

Session	Presentation	Usefulness/ relevance of content	Right level	Enjoyable

Please add any other comments or suggestions that you would like to make:

Example 3

W54

NORFOLK COUNTY COUNCIL
STAFF DEVELOPMENT SCHEME

COURSE EVALUATION FORM

Items 1–7 are to be answered by the course participant and item 8 is to be completed by the participant's Line Manager.

COURSE TITLE:	NAME:
VENUE:	PRESENT JOB TITLE:
DATE(S):	
COURSE ORGANISER(S)	PLACE OF WORK:

Please refer to your declared reasons for wishing to do this course before completing.

1. How do you relate the value of this course to your work? (please tick)

    1.   Of no value

    2.   Of little value

    3.   Valuable

    4.   Very Valuable

2. From the course, have you been able to use in your job:-

    (a)   The knowledge learned (please give details below)

    (b)   The skills acquired/developed (please give details below)

3. (a)   How would you say your attitudes have changed as a result of attending this course?

    (b)   In what way have clients or colleagues been affected by any change in your attitudes?

Data on Computer ....

Example 3 continued

4. In what way is your personal development likely to be influenced as a result of this course.

5. What further needs can you identify as a result of this course. Please comment on how these needs could be met.

6. Please summarise your opinion of the course by grading it in the 1 - 5 scale, ticking in the appropriate box.

	5	4	3	2	1
Adherence to course syllabus					
Supporting Paperwork					
Course Tutor(s)					
Course Administration					

5. Excellent

4. Very Good

3. Good - minor points of detail could have been better.

2. Satisfactory

1. Weak

7. Any Other Comments? e.g. Accommodation

8. COMMENTS FROM LINE MANAGER

Course Members Signature . . . . Date: . . . .

Line Managers Signature . . . . Date: . . . .

Please return this form to the COURSE MANAGER.

Example 4

INSET EVALUATION

Please complete and return this evaluation sheet together with any outstanding relevant claim forms.

Title and dates of activity/activities.

....

....

INSET Reference number:- _____

Have you completed and returned **all** relevant claim forms?   YES / NO

Did the planned activity turn out well in practice?
Refer to organisation, resources and delivery.

....

....

....

....

Comment on the effectiveness of the activity/activities by indicating the extent to which your learning objectives, as stated on your proposal form, were achieved.

....

....

....

....

Indicate any actual or potential changes in your professional practice.
eg. Management styles, teaching and learning styles etc.

....

....

....

....

NORFOLK COUNTY COUNCIL
Education

| Example 4 | continued

Describe and evaluate your dissemination process.

....
....
....

Please attach a copy of any written reports(s).

List any further INSET needs which have been identified by you or your colleagues.

....
....
....

Signature _____   Date _____

> **For the staff development manager of your school.**
>
> How has your service/institution benefited from the INSET activity/activities.
>
>
>
> Signature _____ Date _____

This form should be returned as soon as possible after the
event date(s) to:-
Dr. M Howorth
Assistant Principal (Administration)

City College
NORWICH

CC/JC/DD/91

Example 5

NATIONAL TRAINING INDEX

Audio Visual Training Package appraisal form

The National Training Index, of which your organisation is a member, is seeking information on the quality and effectiveness of training packages. If you will complete this form as fully as possible, it will enable us to give an indication of the likely value of the package to other members of the Index who may be considering using it.

A. THE AUDIO-VISUAL PACKAGE

Title

Supplied by (name of organisation from which the package was bought or hired)

Subject matter

Form in which the visual training material was presented (slides, stills, film)

Did the audio side dovetail easily with the visual material?

Were there sufficient opportunities for trainee involvement?

Cost (please state whether purchase or hire)

B. DATE FIRST USED

C. EVALUATION

1. What were the package's objectives?

2. To what extent did it achieve them? Very well/well/average/only satisfactorily/poorly. (Tick as appropriate.)

3. Were there any particularly good features about the training package? If so, what?

4. Were there any serious shortcomings? What were they?

Example 5 continued

5. Was the technical quality of the package up to standard?

_____

6. For what level of trainee was the package most suitable?

_____

7. Were the instructor's manual and the trainees' material (workbooks, etc.) of a good standard?

_____

8. Any other comments you may like to make:

_____

9. Would you, as a trainer, say that using this training package was an acceptable substitute for sending the trainees concerned on an external training course?

D. THE REVIEWER
_____

Name
_____

Job title
_____

Company/organisation
_____

SIGNATURE   **DATE**
_____

Example 6

NATIONAL TRAINING INDEX

Training Film appraisal form

The National Training Index, of which your organisation is a member, is seeking information on the quality and effectiveness of training films. If you will complete this form as fully as possible, it will enable us to give an indication of the likely value of the film to other members of the Index who may be considering using it.

A. THE FILM

Title

Supplied by (name of organisation from which the film was bought or hired)

Subject matter

Running time

Type (35mm, 16mm etc.)

Black and white / colour

Cost (please state whether purchase or hire)

B. DATE VIEWED

C. EVALUATION

1. What were the film's objectives?

2. To what extent did it achieve them? Very well/well/average/only satisfactorily/poorly. (Tick as appropriate.)

3. Were there any particularly good features in the content of the film? If so, what?

4. Were there any serious shortcomings in the content of the film? What were they?

Example 6 continued

5. Was the technical quality of the film up to standard?

_____

6. For what level of audience was the film most suitable?

_____

7. Was it entertaining as well as instructive?

_____

8. Any other comments you may like to make.

_____

D. THE REVIEWER
_____
Name
_____
Job title
_____
Company/organisation
_____

SIGNATURE   DATE
_____

Example 7

OPEN LEARNING CENTRE - Room 618

EVALUATION FORM

In order to help us to evaluate the effectiveness of your visit and use of The Open Learning Centre (OLC) could you please complete the following form. When you have finished please leave in the "in-tray" on the table. We hope that your visit to the OLC was useful and that you will use the facilities again. Thankyou for your time and assistance.
Sherry Drewett, Ext. 2908.

Details of Visit

DATE: TIME: AM/PM

NAME: DEPT:
                                        TELEPHONE / EXT. No:

Is this your first visit to the OLC? . . . .

What was the purpose of your visit? . . . .
. . . .

Is the visit linked to a training course you are currently on - if "yes" please state which course.

. . . .
. . . .

What materials did you use?

   VIDEO / TV
   COMPUTER PACKAGE
   INTERACTIVE VIDEO PACKAGE
   CASSETTE TAPE
   REFERENCE BOOKS
   WORK BOOKS
   OTHER - Please state what

. . . .
. . . .
. . . .
. . . .

What was the title/s of the materials or resources used?
. . . .
. . . .
. . . .
. . . .

Please continue overleaf. . .

Example 7 continued

Were all your requirements / objectives met by the materials /visit?
FULLY
PRETTY WELL
PARTLY
NOT AT ALL (Please state why)

. . . .
. . . .
. . . .
. . . .

Was the material / resource easy to use and understand?. . . . .
. . . .
. . . .

Did anything particularly help or hinder you learning? (Please give details)
. . . .
. . . .
. . . .
. . . .

Overall feeling about resource:

Will you use the OLC again?. . . . .
. . . .
. . . .

Please write any other comments about the OLC, the facilities and your experience of
using the centre.. . . . .
. . . .
. . . .
. . . .
. . . .
. . . .
. . . .
. . . .
. . . .
. . . .

What are your feelings about the Open Learning Centre as a facility?

Thankyou for your help.

ADDFOL/1&2

Example 8

NATIONAL TRAINING INDEX

In-Company training appraisal form

This form is for completion by the Training Manager/Officer, NOT by individual delegates.

A   The course

Title or Subject

Run by (name of training organisation concerned)

Brief description of syllabus

No. of delegates attending

Names of the lecturers

Fee charged

Where was the course held (please state whether on your company's premises, or at a different location)

Dates and Duration of Course

B   Summary report

It would be most useful if you will summarise your opinion of the course by grading it on a 1-5 scale, ticking in the appropriate box below.

5 = Very good
4 = Good — minor points of detail could be improved
3 = Average
2 = Satisfactory, room for improvement
1 = Weak

	5	4	3	2	1
General achievement of objectives:					
Effectiveness of the lecturers: Name					
Name					
Name					
Preliminary survey work and consultation with company training staff					
Adherence to agreed course syllabus					
Supporting paperwork					
Follow-up proposals					

Please turn over

Example 8 continued

C   Written appraisal

Your answers to the following questions will enable the Index to compile informative in-company training reports. The more detailed your answers, the fuller the reports the Index will be able to submit to members.

1   (a)   What were your requirements from the course for which you engaged the services of the in-company training organisation?
    (b)   To what extent were these achieved?
    (c)   Was the course content what you required? If not, how did it differ?

---

2   (a)   Which were the best parts of the course?
    (b)   What made them so useful?

---

3   Were any parts of the course not up to standard? If so, please give details.

---

4   Were you satisfied with the way in which the organisation set about the training task — the lecturing personnel, methods of instruction, supporting paperwork, use of visual aids, etc?

---

5   . Would you use this training organisation for your in-company training purposes again?

I authorise you to make use of this report to such extent as you may think fit for the purpose of compiling records and other publications of the National Training Index, and to enter as my agent into such agreements with subscribers as you may consider necessary in order to protect me from any legal liability in respect of any inaccuracy or other defect in this report, whether arising through negligence or otherwise.

Signature _____   Date _____

Company/Organisation ....

Job Title ....

Example 9

OUT RISBYGATE BURY ST EDMUNDS SUFFOLK IP33 3RL (0284) 701301

City & Guilds 730
Teaching Practice Observation Sheet

Name of Tutor:	Date:
Course Title:	Time:

Context and relevance of this lesson to the course:

Was the lesson planned? Was it well structured?

Were lesson objectives specified?

Suitable arrangement of the room?

Timing during the session? Atmosphere?

Use of audio-visual aids and handouts:

Was there good teacher/student and student/student communication?

Example 9 continued

Appropriate teaching methods and activities to motivate students?

Was the level appropriate for each student? Any problems?

Were objectives achieved? Did assessment take place?

Other comments and areas for further development

Tutor Self Assessment (continue on a separate sheet if wished)

Signed by Observing Tutor:	Tutor:

Example 10

CCE - COURSE EVALUATION

To help us to maintain a high standard of tuition will you please complete the following assessment of your Course.

Title of course   _____

Date of course   _____

Course delegate's name   _____

Please tick as appropriate.

1   The course content was:

Excellent ❑ Good ❑ Satisfactory ❑ Fair ❑ Poor ❑

2   The standard of tuition and training was:

Excellent ❑ Good ❑ Satisfactory ❑ Fair ❑ Poor ❑

3   The standard of course material and handouts was:

Excellent ❑ Good ❑ Satisfactory ❑ Fair ❑ Poor ❑

4   The facilities and equipment (including accommodation) were:

Excellent ❑ Good ❑ Satisfactory ❑ Fair ❑ Poor ❑

5   The level of treatment was:

Too advanced ❑ About right ❑ Too elementary ❑

6   Was too much time spent on some topics? Which ones?

_____

_____

7   Was too little time spent on some topics? Which ones?

_____

_____

Example 10 continued

8   Were any topics not included which you would have liked included?
     Which ones?

     _____

     _____

9   Were any topics included which you feel could have been left out?
     Which ones?

     _____

     _____

10   Could anything be done to improve the overall standard of the course? If
     so, what would you suggest?

     _____

     _____

     _____

     _____

11   How were you made aware of the course?

     a)   Advertisement in Local Press   ☐

     b)   Advertisement in Journal (please name)   ☐

     c)   Course brochure circulated around office   ☐

     d)   Recommendation from a colleague   ☐

     e)   Other (please state)   ☐

           _____

           _____

     If you would like to learn more about this subject and be considered for a
     place on further courses, please give your name, address and telephone
     number.

     _____

     Thank you for your help.

Example 11

ANGLIA POLYTECHNIC
ADMINISTRATIVE STAFF
STAFF DEVELOPMENT
(Preparation Form)

DEPARTMENT: ....

NAME: ....

PRESENT POST: ....

YEAR UNDER REVIEW: ....

Notes: This form is to assist you in preparing for your forthcoming Staff Development interview. There are two parts:

PART 1 looks back into the past year
PART 2 looks forward to the year ahead

After compleeting the form please send it to the person conducting your interview not less than two weeks before it occurs, keeping a copy for yourself.

PART 1 - THE PAST YEAR

A   Achievements
         Summarise your own assessment of your most significant achievements during the past year.

B   Difficulties/Constraints
         What parts of your job caused you the most difficulties and why?

C   Other Activities
         If there have been other activities related to your job, such as a training course, that you would like your interviewer to know about before the interview, please describe them.

PART 2 - THE YEAR AHEAD

A   Priority Tasks
         Please try and identify what you see as the main tasks related to your post and any innovations you may be considering to improve your performance.

B   Training and Professional Development
         What training or other professional development might help you in the next one to three years, both in performing your job and furthering your career?

C   Other Issues
         Please list any other issues that you would like to discuss during your staff development interview.

Date... Signature ....

Example 12

FORM SD6

ANGLIA POLYTECHNIC
ADMINISTRATIVE STAFF
STAFF DEVELOPMENT
(Report Form)

DEPARTMENT: ....

NAME: ....

PRESENT POST: ....

YEAR UNDER REVIEW: ....
NAME OF INTERVIEWER: ....

PART 1 - THE PAST YEAR

A   Summary of Achievements and Difficulties Encountered in Previous Year

PART 2 - THE YEAR AHEAD

A   Agreed Priority Tasks

B   Recommendations Concerning Training and/or Professional Development

C   Other Issues

PART 3 - ADDITIONAL COMMENTS BY INTERVIEWER

PART 4 - ADDITIONAL COMMENTS BY INTERVIEWEE
           (To include agreement or otherwise to this report)

Signed.. (Interviewee)
Date...

PART 5 - COMMENTS BY SENIOR OFFICER

INTERVIEWER   INTERVIEWEE

Signed ....   Signed ....
Position ....   Position ....
Date ....   Date ....

Index